SdKfz 251 Half-Track 1939–45

Bruce Culver • Illustrated by Bruce Culver and Jim Laurier

First published in Great Britain in 1998 by Osprey Publishing,
Midland House, West Way, Botley, Oxford OX2 0PH, UK
443 Park Avenue South, New York, NY 10016, USA
E-mail: info@ospreypublishing.com

Transferred to digital print on demand 2008

First published 1998
Seventh impression 2007

Printed and bound by PrintOnDemand-Worldwide.com, Peterborough, UK

A CIP catalogue record for this book is available from the British Library

ISBN: 978 1 85532 846 4

Editorial by Marcus Cowper
Design by Rebecca Smart
Index by Alan Thatcher
Colour plates by Bruce Culver
Cutaway artwork by Jim Laurier
Cutaway annotation by Hilary Doyle
Originated by Anglia Graphics

Publisher's note

Readers may wish to study this title in conjunction with the following Osprey publications:

New Vanguard 1 *Kingtiger - Heavy Tank 1942-45*
New Vanguard 5 *Tiger I - Heavy Tank 1942-45*
New Vanguard 15 *Flammpanzer - German Flamethrowers 1941-45*
New Vanguard 19 *Stug III - Assault Gun 1940-42*
New Vanguard 22 *Panther Variants 1942-45*
New Vanguard 26 *German Light Panzers 1932-42*
Men At Arms 24 *Panzer Divisions*
Campaign 5 *Ardennes 1944*
Campaign 16 *Kursk 1943*
Campaign 42 *Operation Bagration*

Editor's note

This book is a revised copy of Vanguard 32 *SdKfz 251 Half-Track*, first published in 1983. The text has been revised,
new black and white photos included and a detailed cutaway of an SdKfz 251/1 Ausf. C added.

Artist's note

Jim Laurier would like to thank the staff of the Patton Museum of Cavalry and Armor, Fort Knox, Kentucky, USA, for
their kind help in suppying reference material for the annotated cutaway. Readers may care to note that copies of the
computer-generated cutaway are available for private sale from the artist. All reproduction copyright whatsoever is
retained by the publishers. Enquiries should be addressed to:

Jim Laurier, PO Box 1118, Keene, NH 03431, USA
http://aviation-arts.simplenet.com

The publishers regret that they can enter into no correspondence upon this matter.

FOR A CATALOGUE OF ALL BOOKS PUBLISHED BY OSPREY
MILITARY AND AVIATION PLEASE CONTACT:

Osprey Direct, c/o Random House Distribution Center,
400 Hahn Road, Westminster, MD 21157
Email: uscustomerservice@ospreypublishing.com

Osprey Direct, The Book Service Ltd, Distribution Centre,
Colchester Road, Frating Green, Colchester, Essex, CO7 7DW
E-mail: customerservice@ospreypublishing.com

www.ospreypublishing.com

SDKFZ 251 HALF-TRACK
1939–1945

DESIGN AND DEVELOPMENT

The efficient use of tanks in modern warfare has in large measure been the result of developments in combat vehicles designed to carry infantry units into action with the tanks, providing close-in support and protection from enemy tank-killer teams. Modern tank armoured infantry formations have evolved over many years; but the first widespread use of armoured infantry to accompany tanks in the assault occurred during the Second World War.

Near the end of the First World War, fairly large tank battles were fought at several places on the Western Front, perhaps the best known being Cambrai. Early tanks, such as the British Mk I–IV and the German A7V, were large, slow, unreliable, and often unwieldy. Nonetheless, to many farsighted front-line officers in both Allied and Central Power armies, these primitive fighting machines had changed the face of land warfare forever. Though most of these young officers were ignored by the entrenched military establishments, they *were* correct: the two major

reasons why the Second World War was so completely different from the First were the development of the military aircraft, and the modern manoeuvrable fighting tank, with the war of rapid movement and concentrated armoured assaults that the tank allowed.

Converted tanks had been used in the First World War to carry supporting infantry with the tank forces, but this was a tactic of expediency, as there was little the infantry could do in their hot iron boxes. After 1918, tank development in the Allied armies generally languished. What little money was spent more often than not went on prototypes of various tank designs. Though some of this effort would pay off in the years ahead, at the time there were very few tanks available. Those that were used in service were assigned to the infantry. Thus, the most common forms of tanks in the 1920s were those intended to advance with the infantry at a walking pace, suppressing enemy defensive fire, and generally limited to a top speed of 10 to 12 mph. Light tanks suitable for scouting or reconnaissance were generally assigned to cavalry units, but were too lightly armoured and armed to function as assault vehicles. In this environment of confusion and specialised, single-purpose vehicles, it is not surprising that relatively little was done to provide armoured vehicles for infantry assaults.

Defeated in 1918, Germany was more successful in overcoming the conservatism of the General Staff, and during the 1920s and early '30s she had conducted numerous experiments with developments in tanks and armoured cars. More importantly, Germany's armour tacticians

An Ausf. A command vehicle of the same company; note that at this early date the tactical sign is still that for motorised rather than armoured infantry. The platform fitted above the driver's position of this modified vehicle is for map-reading.

made far more progress in developing a whole new concept of warfare. Though the British coined the word 'Blitzkrieg', 'lightning war' – a war of movement – was an apt description of the concentrated, co-ordinated armour assault proposed by officers like Heinz Guderian.

With the ascendancy of Adolf Hitler in 1933 and the subsequent rejection of the Treaty of Versailles, Germany concentrated openly on re-armament. The early light tanks, the PzKpfw I and II, were intended only as light reconnaissance vehicles, with the PzKpfw II having a limited rôle in assaults against lightly defended positions. The PzKpfw III and IV, meanwhile, were intended from the start as the main armoured vehicles in the attack.

It was at this point, in 1936-37, that the concept of a specialised vehicle for armoured infantry became more popular. Important combat lessons from the Spanish Civil War showed, among other things, that in many cases tanks in restricted areas – towns, mountain passes, woods, etc. – were vulnerable to enemy anti-tank weapons. In such circumstances, infantry support and protection were badly needed. Guderian submitted proposals to develop a specific vehicle designed to carry supporting infantry into action, allowing them to fight from the vehicle on the move if necessary, or to dismount and engage the enemy on foot. Such a vehicle required a good top speed and good cross-country performance, and had to be cheap enough to build in reasonable numbers.

Since Germany was already producing a large variety of specialised military vehicles, these were considered in the light of the requirement.

An Ausf. A retro-fitted with the MG shield, but retaining the original radio antenna on the mudguard. The individual vehicle number on the nearside mudguard was frequently seen early in the war. This vehicle is emerging from a river crossing in France.

Fully-tracked vehicles were rejected because of the complexity, expense, and lack of current production capacity. A wheeled vehicle design was rejected because cross-country performance would have been inadequate. The search narrowed down to the several types of half-tracked artillery tractors then being produced. Of these, the most suitable for carrying a squad (gruppe) of ten men and their equipment was the SdKfz II 3-tonne artillery tractor developed by Hanomag. Following development, the new 'Mittlerer gepanzerter Mannschafttransportwagen' (MTW) was standardised as the **SdKfz 251 Ausführung A.**

Description

Development of the new vehicle was aided by the fact that very few changes to the SdKfz II chassis were required. The new armoured superstructure designed by Büssing NAG was bolted to the Hanomag chassis frame, an armoured belly plate being bolted onto the frame bottom. The major alteration to the chassis was the use of an angled steering wheel driving the steering gear shaft through a bevel gearbox. The radiator installation was adapted to fit inside the armoured nose section.

The front axle was unpowered, and served only to support the weight of the engine and nose armour. Two pressed steel wheels were mounted on the front axle beam, which was supported by a multi-leaf transverse spring, and braced to the chassis itself by two trailing arms forming an 'A' frame, which was hinged to the chassis at its apex. Two restraining

The 251/4 was a towing vehicle for light artillery, e.g. the 3.7cm PaK36, 7.5cm 1e IG, and 10.5cm 1e FH18. This 251/4 Ausf. A – note 'boxed' 1.Pz-Div sign on left rear hull quarter – towed the 10.5cm howitzer. It retains the earlier crane mount for the front MG 34.

straps limited the front axle drop when the vehicle crossed ditches and other obstacles.

The engine was a Maybach HL42 6-cylinder water-cooled in-line gasoline (petrol) engine of 4.17 litres displacement and developing 100 hp at 2,800 rpm. The powertrain consisted of a Hanomag 021 32 785 U50 transmission with four gears forward and one reverse with a two-speed transfer case giving a total of eight forward speeds and two reverse. Though a fully-tracked design had been rejected because of excessive cost and complexity, the long ground run of the tracks required the use of a tank-type steering final drive unit. During slight turns, the steering wheel turned only the front wheels. Past 15°, the clutch and brake steering mechanism in the final drive system operated to slow the track on the inside of the turn and apply full power to the outside track. Though this was a complexity avoided in the US White M2/M3 half-tracks with their short track ground runs and ordinary truck-type differential drive axles, the cross-country performance of the German armoured troop carrier was excellent, and usually superior to the simpler US types.[1]

The main suspension design was identical to that of the SdKfz II artillery tractor. Each side had a drive sprocket of cast and welded construction, with a rubber rim to carry the tracks, and rollers to engage the guide teeth and drive the tracks. Seven pairs of interleaved pressed steel roadwheels comprised the suspension. Each pair of rubber-tyred

---

1 Though see Vanguard 31, *US Half-Tracks of World War II*, for a contrasting opinion.

wheels was carried on a trailing arm torsion bar. The wheels on the left side were 4ins. farther back than those on the right, since the torsion bars overlapped across the floor of the chassis and had to he offset. Unique to the SdKfz II chassis, the rear pairs of wheels on both sides were also offset, since the rear axles on the 3-tonne chassis were mounted on torsion bars. The track on the right side had 55 shoes while that on the left had 56.

The track consisted of a manganese steel skeleton casting for each shoe. A rubber block was mounted on a raised pad, and a guide tooth, which also engaged the rollers on the drive sprocket, extended from the inner side. The shoes were joined by low-friction needle bearings and steel pins. Though these did require more maintenance than the dry pin tracks used on tanks, the needle bearings allowed the high track speeds necessary to provide the new armoured troop carrier with good cross-country performance to keep up with the tanks. A lubrication fitting was provided in each shoe.

The armoured superstructure was welded from armour plate, and was made in two sections bolted together just aft of the driver's and vehicle commander's seats. The front section protected the engine and powertrain plus the driver and commander. The nose plates were 14.5mm thick, with side and engine deck plates of 9mm and 10mm thickness. The air intake for the radiator was a grille in the engine deck at the front of the nose section. Large double hatches in the engine deck allowed access to the engine and radiator for maintenance, and two additional cooling flaps were provided in the upper side plates over the front mudguards. A third cooling flap was located in the lower nose plate.

The vehicle crew was protected by front and side armour 8mm thick

**SdKfz 251/1 Ausf. A
(© H.L. Doyle)**

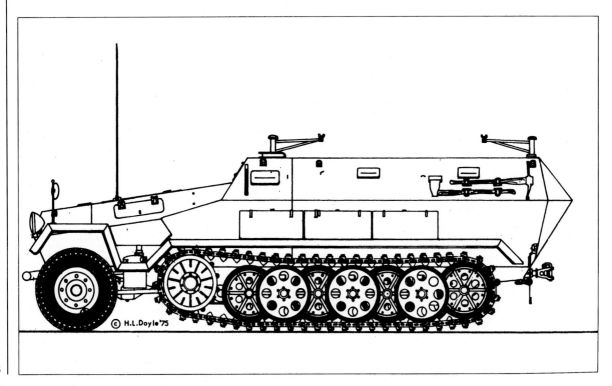

251/10 Ausf. A, bearing the 'inverted Y' sign which replaced the 1.Pz-Div.'s oakleaf for Operation 'Barbarossa', and fitted with an intermediate type of armoured shield for the PaK 36 3.7cm gun. The whole shield moved with the gun, and the side extensions gave added protection to the crew and commander.

and by a roof of 8mm plate. Removable floor plates under the front seats allowed access to the battery and chassis, and the transmission and final drive units were enclosed beneath the floor. The original front seats had padded cushions and separate backrest cushions with single support frames. On the front bulkhead were the driver's controls: steering wheel; clutch, brake and accelerator pedals; the transmission and transfer case levers, parking brake lever, and driving instruments. In front of the vehicle commander's right front seat was a container for medical supplies. A Funksprechgerät 'F' radio telephone set was mounted on the side wall above and behind the right front seat. It was somewhat inconvenient, and required the commander to twist in his seat to operate the controls.

Vision ports in the front and side plates allowed the crew a measure of protected vision. In rear areas and convoys, the entire armour visor could be raised. In areas where fire could be expected, the armour plate section of the visor could be raised, leaving the thick armour glass vision block to protect the crew. In front-line areas the metal visor was lowered to provide better protection, though at the cost of reduced vision. Spare glass blocks were carried to replace those damaged by shell splinters.

The rear section carried the infantry squad, and was essentially a long open-topped box with seats for ten men. The upper and lower sides were 8mm plate, and were angled to provide better ballistic protection. At the front end a prominent flange was welded to the side plates, and the rear section was then bolted to the front. At the back, angled rear and corner plates enclosed the crew compartment, with two large exit doors in the centre. The doors were built up from two pieces of plate bolted together, and were mounted on hinged swing-out arms. There was a narrow top crosspiece bolted to the body rear plates to close off the top of the door opening. A towing pintle was mounted in the centre of the rear hull below the doors, and an electrical connection and compressed air brake line for towed trailers, etc., were provided at the lower left of the rear body.

The interior arrangement in this early model was very simple. Four bench seats, two along each side, provided seating for the crew. The seats folded upwards to allow access to the ten boxes of machine gun ammunition stowed beneath each seat in floor brackets. There were no seat backs, and brackets on the side walls allowed for the stowage of rifles, two MG34s, spare barrels, a heavy mount for one of the MG34s, and carriers at the rear for 50-round ammunition drums for the guns. Two fixed vision ports were provided in each upper side wall.

Initial armament was a pair of MG34 light machine guns on swing-out crane-type mounts for anti-aircraft and ground fire. A number of vehicles were assigned to heavy machine gun sections, and these carried two heavy tripods on the forward side walls just behind the body joint flange. Heavy MG section vehicles also had a heavy tripod mount fitting for the front MG34. This allowed the gun to be used for relatively

accurate long-range suppression fire. The SdKfz 251 Ausf. A entered service trials in 1939, and some saw service in the Polish campaign.

A larger number of vehicles were on hand to equip part of the 1st Schützen (Rifle) Regiment of the 1st Panzer Division during the campaign in the West in the spring of 1940.

Heavily 'stowed' with the packs of the crew, ammunition boxes, and the spare tracks which were often used as appliqué armour, a 251/1 Ausf. B of 7. Panzer-Division rolls on into Russia during the invasion of summer 1941.

VARIANTS

Early combat experience led to improvements. An interim model, the **Ausf. B**, incorporated few changes, but did eliminate the view ports in the rear body sides and re-organised the stowage and some internal fittings. Externally it was almost identical to the Ausf. A. A new front MG mount with an armoured shield and a fixed pivot mount improved protection for the gunner and made the gun more accurate. The rear crane mount was retained, primarily for anti-aircraft use. The new mount was also widely retrofitted to Ausf. As. The Ausf. B also had the FuSpG 'F' R/T antenna moved from the right front mudguard back to the right upper side over the radio. Late Ausf. Bs had some improvements officially introduced on the Ausf. C.

The first version to take full advantage of the experience gained in trials and early combat was the SdKfz 251 **Ausf. C**. The most noticeable improvements in the Ausf. C were in the design of the engine compartment armour layout, and the crew's interior stowage and seating arrangements. The engine section was extensively modified.

A single-piece 14.5mm nose plate replaced the original two-piece design. The cooling air was now drawn up behind the lower front plate, the open top grille being eliminated. The side cooling flaps were replaced with side vent cover boxes, which allowed the vents to remain open all the time for better cooling.

The forward sections of the main suspension mudguards were raised at the front to provide more clearance between the drive sprockets and the mudguards: there had been instances of heavy mud and debris fouling the original straight mudguards. Pioneer tools were removed from the upper rear sides of the body and placed on the front part of the track mudguards. The side stowage bins were moved to the rear to allow room for the mudguard modifications and tool stowage.

The interior stowage and seating arrangements were completely reworked. So successful were these modifications that they remained standard for the rest of the war. The seats were built in sections, each forward seat accommodating three men and the rear seats two. The bottom of each seat comprised a floor-mounted stowage bin with a removable top and a front access flap. The seat frames were welded, formed steel tubing with heavy, flat springs, covered with horsehair-padded leather cushions. The driver's and commander's seats were also redesigned, having a tubular frame with flat springs to support the seat and back cushions.

The equipment and weapons stowage was also new. The FuSpG 'F' R/T was moved under the front armour in front of the commander's seat, where the medical kit had been. Map tubes were usually provided

11

behind the R/T set, and an optional hot air heating duct could be found on the forward bulkhead.

Stowage in the rear body compartment was altered to improve accessibility to weapons and equipment. All the side wall stowage brackets and fittings were attached to a false inner wall bolted to the external armour plates. New racks were provided to stow the Kar 98k service rifles, four on each side. A heavy flap in front of each rack folded down for access to the rifles. When raised, it served as a backrest for the soldiers in the front seat, and had a horsehair-filled leather cushion. To the rear of each rifle rack was a stowage bin open at the top. A seat backrest cushion was fastened on the front side for the men in the rear seat. On the rear corner plates were carriers for 50-round ammo drums for the MG34s, and spent case sacks to catch empty cartridges during firing. Behind the seats, on the lower side walls, were brackets for stowing two MG34 light machine guns and spare barrel containers. This proved to be a most efficient layout and, though altered or adapted for special-purpose variants, it remained the standard armoured infantry carrier configuration for the rest of the war. The rear doors were formed from single pieces of plate, bent to match the body angles. The door hinge mounts were welded to the armour plates; not bolted as was previously done.

One of the greatest problems the Germans had during the early part of the war was a lack of production capacity actually available to the war effort, and the resulting shortages of vehicles, which often made it necessary to scale down or delay re-equipment programmes. Early belief in the likelihood of a short war led to inadequate plans for production and procurement as the war dragged on. Germany's war machine had not been geared to produce the large quantities of material needed for an extended conflict. In 1940 several additional firms were brought into the SdKfz 251 programme to increase the supply of these critically needed vehicles. Because many of these companies had no experience of welding homogeneous armour plate, an alternative riveted body structure was developed; this could be produced until the necessary training and experience in welding techniques were acquired. A number of the SdKfz 251 Ausf. C vehicles thus had a riveted structure, with the engine cooling vent covers formed from the upper side armour pieces, instead of being welded boxes added to the straight side plates. In other respects, these vehicles were the same as the welded versions.

In early 1941 the SdKfz 251 was officially redesignated as 'mittlerer Schützenpanzerwagen' (medium armoured infantry carrier), usually abbreviated as 'SPW'

Planning for the establishment of the Panzer Divisions had also thrown up requirements for a variety of special-purpose vehicles for support and command functions. Because the SdKfz 251 was relatively spacious and had the necessary cross-country performance the army decided to use special versions of the 251 to meet the need for these special vehicles. This also relieved pressures on tank production – tanks were the only real alternatives – and simplified logistics.

This shot of a 251/1 Ausf. B with PzKpfw IB tanks has been captioned as showing vehicles commited to the invasion of Greece, 1941 – this seems most unlikely, given the configuration of the vehicles, and it probably shows tank co-operation training.

This 251/3 of 5.Leichte-Division, DAK carries the type of 'expedient' camouflage of mud over factory grey often seen during the early months of the Afrikakorps' operations. Behind it is one of the captured AEC Dorchester command vehicles used by Rommel and his staff.

Each version of the SdKfz 251 was identified by a slash (/) and a number, followed by the Aüsführung designation of the basic body. The basic 'Schützenpanzerwagen' (SPW) – the armoured infantry personnel carrier – was designated SdKfz 251/I Ausf. A, B, or C (depending on the vehicle's model). This designation was very specific and allowed the supply personnel to choose the correct spares from stocks held by units in the field. The vehicle for the heavy machine gun section, with its special forward gun mount, was referred to as **SdKfz 251/I** (s.MG) Ausf. A (or B or C).

The initial support and command versions of the SdKfz 251 were developed in 1939-40. **The SdKfz 251/2** provided a mobile mount for the 8cm GrW34 medium mortar and crew. A baseplate was stowed in the vehicle so that the mortar could be fired from the ground, with the vehicle used as an ammunition carrier. When firing the mortar from the vehicle, the driver would stop the half-track, the mortar crew would aim the weapon, and then fire as with a ground-mounted weapon. The advantage of having the SdKfz 251/2 was that the mortar could be moved rapidly without trouble, making it more versatile and protecting the crew from enemy fire. The forward MG34 was removed.

The **SdKfz 251/3** was a communications vehicle carrying several radio sets. There were several versions, all differing in the complement of radios. Some were used for infantry command and co-ordination, some for armoured units, still others for Luftwaffe ground-air communications. All of the /3 versions had a prominent built-up antenna with a perimeter frame and a raised centre spine. Some command and liaison vehicles equipped with Fu- II were also fitted with a collapsible nine-metre sectional rod antenna. From 1942, the frame antenna was often replaced with a 'star' rod antenna, which was not so conspicuous.

The **SdKfz 251/4** was a towing vehicle for the 10.5cm le FH18 medium howitzer. It also carried the crew and a small amount of ammunition. After the crew set up the gun and began their fire mission, the half-track served as an ammunition carrier. This version was eventually replaced as a 10.5cm howitzer tractor by the Wespe self-propelled howitzer. Because of the shortage of self-propelled anti-tank weapons, however, variations of the SdKfz 251/4 were used to the end of the war to tow the 5cm PaK38 and later the 7.5cm PaK40.

Armoured assaults often involved advancing through anti-tank obstacles, and all Panzer Divisions had assault engineers (pioneers) to accompany the tanks to clear mines and obstacles, fill in anti-tank ditches and craters, and repair bridges. It was obvious that the pioneer companies would need armoured vehicles, and the **SdKfz 251/5** was designed as a specialised carrier for a heavy assault pioneer section. The interior stowage was extensively altered to carry the special equipment used by pioneer troops. The exact layout varied, as units in some areas and climates required equipment and supplies different from those used in other areas. The standard armament of two MG34s was retained.

The **SdKfz 251/6** was a variant of the SdKfz 251/3, but fitted out for the use of senior commanders. It carried the same basic command radio sets as a SdKfz 251/3 of the same unit, but in addition the /6 carried cryptographic decoding equipment (the Enigma machine) and extra radio operators. Most of the SdKfz 251 /6s were converted from Ausf. A vehicles. Some of these command vehicles had no armament. In many cases, the easiest way to identify the /6 variant is to note the presence of command pennants and markings on the front plate, or the presence of well-known senior commanders in the vehicles.

The **SdKfz 251/7** was a less extensively modified pioneers' vehicle than the /5, and was intended for a light assault pioneer section. More of the original vehicle layout was retained, the major change being the addition of extra brackets for specialised equipment. There were two models of the SdKfz 251/7, designated types I and II: they were similar, differing only in stowage. Equipment carried varied as for the /5, from chainsaws to pyrotechnics and demolitions equipment. Both MG34s were retained, and two assault bridge treadways were also carried. A number of pioneer units re-arranged the bridge brackets in order to place boards between them, providing extra stowage areas for crew equipment. The SdKfz 251/7 was produced in greater numbers than the /5, and gradually supplanted the earlier vehicle.

Many nations evolved armoured ambulances for recovering wounded personnel from front-line combat areas. The **SdKfz 251/8** was designed as an armoured field ambulance suitable for four stretcher cases or up to ten sitting wounded. The normal seats and equipment brackets were removed and replaced with folding stretchers and seats. All armament was removed, and large Red Cross markings were applied as per the provisions of the Geneva Convention. A water container was situated

SdKfz 251/1 Ausf. C.
(© H.L. Doyle)

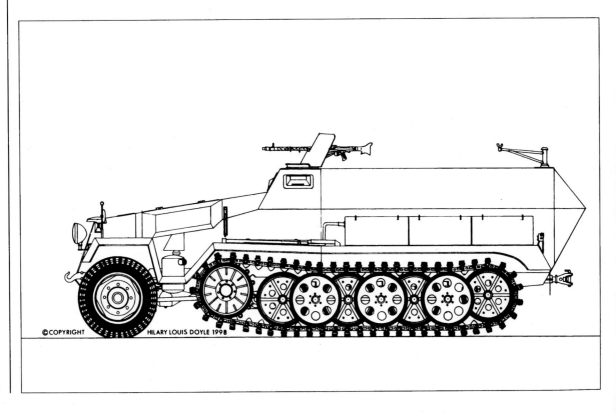

©COPYRIGHT HILARY LOUIS DOYLE 1998

over the transmission housing, and medical supplies were carried. Because of the shortage of SdKfz 251/8s, a number of standard /1 personnel carriers were converted for ambulance duty by removing the MG34s and applying Red Cross markings or flying a Red Cross flag. The extemporaneous ambulances usually can be identified by the presence of the forward MG armour shield, without the gun. The true /8 ambulance had the entire mount removed and, in addition, the rear top plate was often removed so that stretchers could be carried from the vehicle more easily.

The **SdKfz 251/9** was designed to provide close fire support for reconnaissance units. The rearming of the PzKpfw IV Ausf. F with the KwK40 L/43 long gun provided a number of 7.5cm KwK37 L/24 howitzers originally intended for those tanks. Additional L/24 howitzers became available as earlier PzKpfw IVs were rebuilt with long guns. The SdKfz 251/9 carried the howitzer in the mount originally developed for the StuG III assault gun. The cradle base was bolted to the floor frame, and the right hand portion of the driver's compartment was cut away to provide clearance for the gun. Traverse was very limited, but adequate, since the rough aiming was done by positioning the entire vehicle to face the target. The crew was four men, and the rear crane-mounted MG34 was retained. The FuSpG 'F' R/T set was moved to the left side wall, and an ammunition bin replaced the left rear seat. Fifty-two rounds of ammunition were carried, with six rounds in a ready rack on the right wall near the howitzer.

Even with the very heavy squad firepower from several MG34s, the Germans found a need for a heavier support weapon for the attacking infantry. The **SdKfz 251/10** was issued to platoon leaders in armoured infantry companies, and mounted a 3.7cm PaK36 light anti-tank gun.

Early models mounted not only the gun but also the large shield used on the field mount. Since the crew was protected by the vehicle and the shield was very high, lower shields were soon developed to protect the crew without making the vehicle so conspicuous. The first lower shield went across the front of the gun mount the full width of the vehicle. The second, more common type had a single pair of spaced plates protecting only the gunner. Ammunition was carried in standard containers stored on the right side. Early in the war the 3.7cm PaK36 was still a creditable anti-tank gun, and its HE projectiles were capable of inflicting damage and casualties on unarmoured vehicles or buildings at normal ranges. It proved to be most valuable as a close-in support weapon.

'Field mods' were common; this 251/7 Ausf. C engineers' half-track has been retro-fitted as a command vehicle with a salvaged aerial array from another type of AFV. Damaged mudguards were often removed. note the magnetic anti-tank mines – 'sticky bombs' – on the roof of this half-track.

By 1940, it had been decided to use the SdKfz 251 as the basis for all special-purpose vehicles used by armoured formations; the pace of development and conversion picked up, and numerous variants were developed for different units in the Panzer Divisions. The **SdKfz 251/11** was a telephone communications vehicle used for laying and servicing telephone and telegraph lines and cables. It had a crew of four, and carried cables and telephone lines on reels, together with splicing and servicing equipment.

The **SdKfz 251/12**, **/13**, **/14**, and **/15** were specialised artillery surveying and spotting vehicles. Little is known of the technical details of equipment and stowage, and production was diverted to other versions with higher priorities.

The SdKfz 251/12 carried an artillery surveying section and its instruments. The /13 was a sound-recording vehicle. The SdKfz 251/14 (a sound ranging vehicle) and /15 (a flash-spotting vehicle) were used to detect and plot the location of enemy artillery. In many units these functions were taken over by special-purpose trucks.

The **SdKfz 251/16** was a flamethrower half-track intended for the close support role. The SdKfz 251/16, built on the Ausf. C chassis, carried two 14mm flamethrowers, one on each side, and one 7mm portable flame projector attached to the vehicle by a hose 10 metres long. This small unit was used in cases in which the large projectors could not be aimed properly at a target. Since the portable unit was used outside the vehicle, supporting infantry were required to suppress any defensive fire from the target. Fuel tanks for the flame projectors were mounted along the rear side walls, and the fuel tank for the portable flamethrower was mounted in front of the rear doors, which were kept shut.

During 1941 and 1942 combat experience suggested the need for organic self-propelled anti-aircraft guns to protect armoured formations. Heavy anti-aircraft guns were usually manned by

11.Panzer-Division was very active on the Eastern Front. This 251/3 Ausf. C carries both 'official' and 'unofficial' divisional signs just visible among the scruffy winter camouflage paint on the nose; the vertically-halved yellow circle, and the white 'ghost'.

251/6 Ausf. C of Panzergrenadier-Regt. 'Grossdeutschland' commander, Oberst Lorenz, photographed in 1943; Lorenz is seen at right in vehicle, with goggles on service cap. Note the white divisional sign of 'GD' on the nose plate, the command flag in grey and white, and '01' on hull side.

Luftwaffe crews, since Flak units were under the control of the Luftwaffe, though there were some Heeresflak (Army flak) units to supplement them. Defence against low-level attack was a more pressing need, as tanks were more vulnerable to such tactics. Initially, SdKfz 10/4 and /5 light artillery tractors, mounting the 2cm Flak 30 and Flak 38 respectively, were used for this rôle. Largely unarmoured, these light flak vehicles proved vulnerable not only to enemy aircraft but also to ground fire.

As a field expedient a number of SdKfz 251/1 personnel carriers were converted to anti-aircraft vehicles by mounting 2cm Flak 38 guns inside the rear body. Because of the narrow width of the SdKfz 251 crew compartment, these had only limited traverse, and generally were not suitable for engaging ground targets. Nonetheless, they were useful for air defence and provided better protection for the crew than the open mounts on the SdKfz 7 and SdKfz 10 tractors mounting 2cm and 3.7cm weapons.

In 1942 the Luftwaffe developed a special antiaircraft version of the SdKfz 251 Ausf. C. Ten armed vehicles and two command vehicles with frame antennae were built for troop service trials, and served for a time in Russia. The body was extensively modified, being widened across the crew compartment to allow full traverse for the 2cm Flak 38. The gun was installed on the complete ground mount inside the vehicle above the floor. For engaging ground targets, the sides of the vehicle could be lowered to allow maximum gun depression to the sides. This also reduced the protection for the gun crew, but the 2cm gun could be used effectively at ranges greater than the limits of Russian return fire.

Though practical, this vehicle was considerably more expensive to manufacture, and it was not put into series production. The trial vehicles were extensively photographed, leading to the belief that they were used widely in active service. The two command vehicles had the extensive body modifications although they did not mount the 2cm Flak 38.

During late 1942 and early 1943 it became obvious that far higher production levels of armament would be required to fight a war on several fronts – the vast Russian Front swallowed whole armies, and was the logistic equivalent of several European campaigns. The Deutsches Afrikakorps also required supplies to tie down the divisions of British and Commonwealth troops Hitler wanted kept in Africa and away from any preparations for a war in Europe. Hitler's new armaments minister, Albert Speer, sought ways to diversify and expand production within the limitations of Germany's economy and industry.

The SdKfz 251 employed a body composed of many angled plates, which were time-consuming to cut and assemble. A major redesign of the basic body of the SdKfz 251 resulted in the Ausführung D, which was to be the last basic body variant, Many of the special-purpose versions of the Ausf. A, B, and C were continued with the Ausf. D, while some were eliminated and new ones added. More Ausf. D vehicles were built than all the previous versions together, though early vehicles were often used right up to the end of the war

The primary goal in the design of the **SdKfz 251 Ausf. D** was to increase production. This was achieved by reducing the number of body plates by 50 per cent and simplifying many details of the design. The primary changes in the body were the new engine upper side plates, which eliminated the welded air vent boxes; the stowage bins built into two long boxes on the lower sides; and the straight rear overhang with two straight hinged doors replacing the complex angled 'clamshell' type of the Ausf. A to C. Most pioneer tools were moved to the stowage bins, the pick and axe being placed on the front wheel mudguards. Since the early engine lower side plates were bent to shape, the Ausf. D introduced a new design welded from smaller plates – welding was considered preferable to the special processing required to bend armour plate accurately. The MG34s were replaced by MG42s, but the mounts were otherwise unchanged from the earlier models.

The interior was the same as that of the Ausf. C, and retained all the seats, rifle racks, bins and interior stowage. Improvements and alterations were made to save time or conserve critical materials. The rifle rack buttplate holders were made from wood rather than metal. The crew seats were made of wood slats, much like a park bench, replacing the complex Ausf. C seats with their steel tube frames, springs, and padded leather cushions. The rear doors swung down and out on simple hinges and were locked by internal bars through guides welded

251 Ausf. C of an armoured infantry platoon of Panzergrenadier-Division 'Grossdeutschland' in action in Russia during September 1943, when the division was being ground down in fierce defensive fighting on the southern flank of the great Russian advance after the Kursk battles. Note cross on rear hull; prominent white divisional sign on door; 'crow's-foot' antenna; and three-colour camouflage paint scheme, in an obviously flamboyant pattern.

to the body above and below the door opening. A 'T'-handle outside allowed the rear doors to be locked closed from outside the vehicle – unlike the Ausf. A to C doors, the Ausf. D doors could not be kept closed without locking them. The machine gun stowage brackets were redesigned to accommodate the MG42's bulky square barrel jacket. The special-purpose versions of the Ausf. D were expanded to nearly 20 variants.

Surviving from the earlier Ausf. A to C were the /1 APC, /2 mortar carrier, and the /3 radio vehicle (usually, but not always, with the rod antenna). The SdKfz 251/4 Ausf. D was used to tow the 7.5cm PaK40 in units which lacked sufficient self-propelled AT guns. The SdKfz 251/5 does not appear to have been manufactured on the D chassis, but pioneer troops were well-equipped to alter their own vehicles, and no doubt variations of the /7 Ausf. D pioneer vehicle did exist. It is also possible that some of the Ausf. Ds seen with frame antennae – often field modifications to replace or supplement the rod antennae – were equipped as /6 senior command vehicles with cryptographic sets. As mentioned, the /7 pioneer version appears to have been the factory-built variant for the engineers. The /8 ambulance was very similar to the /8 built on the Ausf. C chassis, and featured the same folding stretchers and seats, and crews still deleted the rear top plate on some vehicles.

The SdKfz 251/9 Ausf. D was built in two versions. The first used the original StuG III L/24 howitzer mount identical to that of the Ausf. C. In late 1943 a new light 7.5cm howitzer mount was developed specifically for converting existing vehicles. It was mounted on the driver's roof plate and required no extensive alterations to the basic body. The L/24 howitzer could be traversed to the limits of the mount, and a co-axial MG42 was mounted next to the main armament for defensive fire. A sight was located to the left of the howitzer, which was aimed and fired

SPWs of the 'Grossdeutschland' Division face the cruel winter horizon at the turn of 1943-44. In the last two months of 1943 the Wehrmacht was forced back 150 miles right across a 650-mile front. That this retreat was in some sectors orderly and costly for the Red Army was largely due to the efforts of mobile battle groups of tanks and half-tracks, which were moved from one weak point to another as 'fire brigades'.

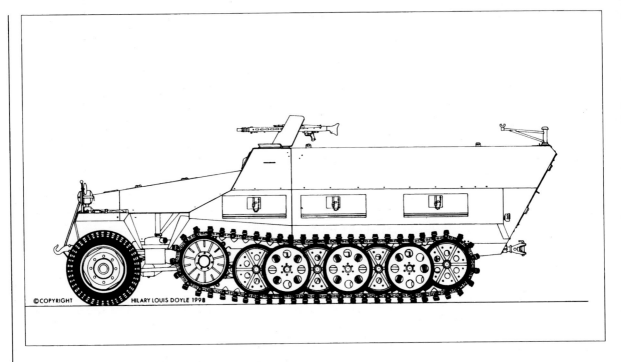

© COPYRIGHT   HILARY LOUIS DOYLE 1998

as for previous models. Thin armour plates protected the front and sides of the mount from shell splinters and fragments. This same mount was also used on the SdKfz 234/3 and SdKfz 250/8 (new body type).[1] Nicknamed 'Stummel' ('Stump'), the SdKfz 251/9 Ausf. D was an effective close-support weapon, and was issued to armoured reconnaissance units.

Relatively few SdKfz 251/10 Ausf. Ds were built, as 1943 combat conditions required heavier weapons than the 3.7cm PaK36. Nonetheless, the /10 Ausf. D was used in some numbers in 1943-44. The SdKfz 251/11 was similar to the earlier version. The SdKfz 251/12-15 appear to have been dropped prior to introduction of the Ausf D body, but a few may have been produced.

The SdKfz 251/17 Ausf. D was an anti-aircraft half-track, the first officially designated anti-aircraft version of the SdKfz 251. This vehicle mounted a single 2cm Flak 38 in a small armoured turret mounted on a pedestal. The gunner sat in a suspended seat behind the weapon and operated the mount by handwheels. The gun was loaded with 20-round box magazines. The crew was four and an MG42 was retained for additional firepower. The single 2cm Flak 38 did not lay down a heavy volume of fire, and the box magazine system required a loader, who was cramped under the vehicle roof. Several of these vehicles were encountered by Allied troops in Europe in late 1944–45.

The **SdKfz 251/18** appears to have been converted from earlier models, and served as an artillery observation post and command vehicle. The main identifying characteristic of the /18 was the large map table built up over the driver's roof plate. The available photos generally show Ausf. A and B vehicles, but some Ausf. C types may have been converted as the need arose.

---

[1]See also the forthcoming title New Vanguard 29, *German Armoured Cars and Reconnaissance Half-Tracks 1939-45*.

Ausf. C *Pionierpanzerwagen* fitted with a 3.7cm 'door-knocker' in place of the forward MG34.

The **SdKfz 251/19** was a mobile telephone exchange vehicle and contained telephone switchboard and routing equipment. These vehicles were built on Ausf. C chassis as well as Ausf. Ds, and were very valuable for maintaining telephone communications in fluid combat situations in which headquarters units were forced to move fairly frequently to maintain contact with the forward areas.

The **SdKfz 251/20** was developed on the Ausf. D body, and mounted a large (60cm) infra red searchlight This vehicle, known as 'Uhu' ('Owl') was used to illuminate targets at night, and worked with Panther tanks equipped with infra red detection equipment. The driver of the SdKfz 251/20 was equipped with an infra red scope, enabling him to see the surrounding area illuminated by the IR searchlight. Though the war ended before regular units were equipped with infra red equipment, the few engagements fought by the IR-equipped Panthers proved the tremendous advantages of this new night-time fighting technique. Several SdKfz 251/20 vehicles were captured, and interest and development in IR sighting has continued up to the present time.

The **SdKfz 251/21** represented a cheaper, more expedient attempt at a new anti-aircraft vehicle, and proved to be the most effective AA version of the SdKfz 251. There were field modifications made on Ausf. C vehicles which approximated the /21, but all production vehicles were built on the Ausf. D chassis.

The interior fittings – rifle racks, front and rear seats, etc. – were removed and a modified naval pedestal mount carrying three 15cm MG 151 aircraft machine guns was mounted on the floor where the front seats had been. The Kriegsmarine had developed the 'Flakdrilling Sockellafette' (triple AA gun mount) as an inexpensive close air defence gun installation. As the Luftwaffe required heavier calibre guns, large quantities of the excellent Mauser 15mm MG 151 were made available for other purposes. In 1944, additional quantities of 2cm MG 151/20 machine guns also became available as the Luftwaffe increased the use of 3cm cannon. Both 15cm and 2cm (20mm) MG 151s were used in the SdKfz 251/21.

The mounting consisted of a fixed base plate with a rotating conical pedestal extending up to the cradle assembly. The cradle held all three MG 151s in aircraft-type buffer assemblies. The guns were mounted offset toward the right side to allow clearance for the belts and feed chutes. The ejected shell cases and belt links were collected in the central pedestal. Three chests of ammunition were carried on the pedestal and rotated with the entire mount. The centre chest held 400 rounds of mixed HE, tracer, and AP ammunition. The outer chests each held 250 rounds. The centre chest was larger because the middle gun was more difficult to reload

The gunner sat on a metal seat suspended from the rear of the gun mount, and moved the entire mount manually; there were no gear drives or handwheels. Two handgrips, one on each side of the mount, contained triggers for firing the guns. Early gun mounts used a reflector-type optical sight, but later versions used a simpler speed ring sight. Later vehicles also had different armour around the guns and cradle assembly.

Additional armour was added to the body of the vehicle across the rear edge of the driver's roof, and along the forward upper edges of the sides. Brackets were provided for a rear armour brace across the body behind the gunner, but this was generally removed. Ammunition was carried in chests at the rear of the vehicle. Total capacity was 3,000 rounds per vehicle. The rear MG42 was retained for vehicle defence.

Perhaps the greatest irony in the development self-propelled AA gun mounts is that such vehicles usually lightly armoured, became the prime targets for enemy fighter-bombers, and the majority of SdKfz 251/21 vehicles lost on the Western Front were destroyed by Allied air attacks. As spare parts and fuel became harder to obtain, many were abandoned and captured virtually intact.

The last major variant of the SdKfz 251 resulted from a personal order by Hitler that all suitable types of vehicles were to be used to mount anti-tank guns. The SdKfz 251 chassis, though somewhat overloaded, was capable of mounting the 7.5cm PaK 40. Vehicles were converted in late1944-early 1945, and issued as the **SdKfz 251/22 Ausf. D**. The mounting was essentially similar to that of the SdKfz 234/4 armoured car, which also carried the PaK 40. Two 'I' beams extended from the rear of the driver's roof plate down and to the rear at an angle, being welded directly to the floor at their lower ends. A platform was welded to the beams partway down from the roof, and the upper carriage of the PaK 40 – comprising the traversing and elevating mechanisms, gun tube, sight, and shield – was bolted to this platform. The lower corners of the gun shield were cut away to clear the sides of the half-track. A section of the driver's roof plate was cut back to clear

251s were often adapted to carry rocket projectiles for infantry support fire. The conversion involved only the fitting of a welded tube assembly upon which vertical baseplates were fixed, each bearing a launcher-support for elevation. The 28cm HE or 32cm napalm projectiles were shipped in crates which doubled as launcher-frames; they were clamped onto the launcher-plates on the baseplates, and the rockets were fired from inside them. Of the two types of crate, the heavy wooden variety (opposite top) were normally discarded after firing; the alternative iron type (bottom right) were sometimes re-used. The photos above and above right show the two vertical vanes fixed to the vehicles' nose as rudimentary sights. Note that the half-track in the left hand photo – in common with many of these *Schützenpanzerwagen mit Wurframen* – bears the tactical sign of an armoured engineer company, with a 'double arrowhead' rising from the 'box'.

the recoil mechanism below the barrel. A simple cradle-type travel lock was welded to the front of the driver's roof. Both front seats and rifle racks were removed.

Two closed ammunition bins were provided near the gun mount. A large bin designed to fit against the right side wall held 17 rounds, and a smaller vertical bin below the mount platform held five rounds. This bin layout made rapid exit from the driver's seat rather difficult, as there was no other way out. The right front (vehicle commander's) seat was eliminated. Loose ammunition in containers below the floor replaced the right rear seat. The left stowage bin and rear seat were retained for the two loaders. The gunner sat in a folding wooden seat to the left of the gun, and aimed and fired the weapon using the standard optical sight for the PaK 40. The position formerly occupied by the left rifle rack was used on some vehicles to stow additional loose ready ammunition. The rear MG42 was retained for vehicle defence.

There has been one reference to the **SdKfz 251/23**, a reconnaissance vehicle intended to replace the SdKfz 250/9, which was withdrawn from production in the 1945 industrial plan. There is no information if any were built or saw service. The description indicates that the SdKfz 251/23 mounted the same 'Hanglafette 38' six-sided turret used on the SdKfz 234/1 and Aufklpz.38(t), mounting a 2cm KwK38 and an MG34. Presumably the entire body was roofed over, as on the SdKfz 250/9.

A widely used modification to the SdKfz 251 APC was fitted with launchers for 28cm or 32cm rocket-propelled projectiles carrying warheads of high explosive (28cm Würfkorper) or jellied petrol (32cm Würfkorper). Two aiming rods were attached at the front of the engine compartment to guide the driver in aiming the vehicle at the target. Elevation was adjustable on the launcher baseplates. Six launcher brackets were used on the SdKfz 251.

The launcher fittings on the SdKfz 251 held wooden or metal frames which were shipped with each projectile, serving as shipping crates during transport. The wooden crates were disposed of when damaged, but the metal frames were reusable. Normally, the rockets were fired while the crew was out of the vehicle, as there was considerable backblast from these spin-stabilised projectiles. The effective range of the rocket projectiles was 1,900 to 2,200 metres, and they were very widely used in reducing built-up areas or enemy fortifications, especially when sufficient artillery support was not available.

Troops in the field excel at adapting to local conditions, and many field modifications appeared in answer to their needs. Most of the 2cm Flak 38 mounts in SdKfz 251s were field-built conversions and many vehicles were temporarily modified, or simply assigned, as ambulances, ammunition and supply carriers, radio and command vehicles, etc. This accounts for many of the odd vehicles that occasionally appear in photographs.

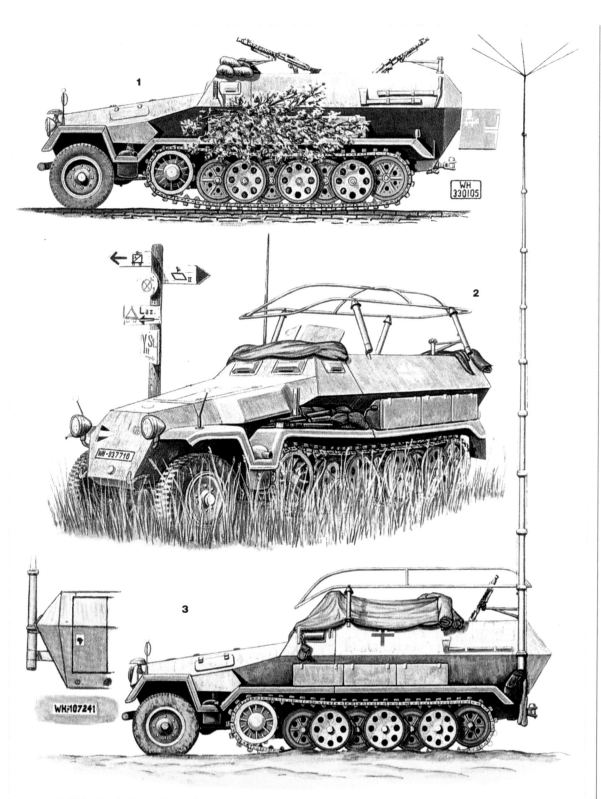

1: SdKfz 251/1 Ausf. A, 10th Co., Schützen-Regt. 1, 1.Panzer-Division; France, 1940
2: SdKfz 251/6 Ausf. C, HQ 9.Panzer-Division; Russia, 1941
3: SdKfz 251/3 Ausf. B; Luftwaffe 'Flivo', Deutsches Afrikakorps, 1942

A

1: SdKfz 251/3 Ausf. B With 2.8cm Panzerbuchse; 3.Panzer-Division, Russia, 1942
2: SdKfz 251/1 Ausf. C, 24.Panzer-Division; Russia, 1942

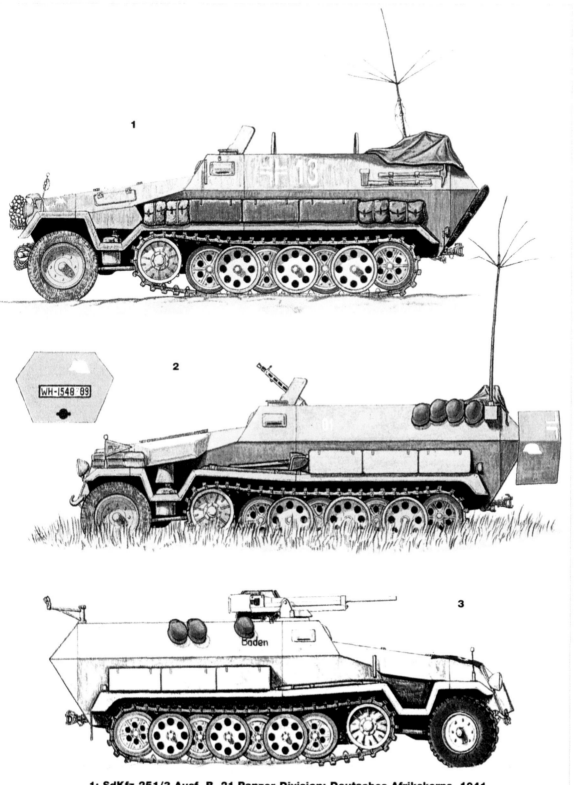

1: SdKfz 251/3 Ausf. B, 21.Panzer-Division; Deutsches Afrikakorps, 1941
2: SdKfz 251/6 Ausf. C, CO of Pz.Gren.Regt., 'Grossdeutschland'; Russia, 1943
3: SdKfz 251/10 Ausf. C, unidentified unit; North Russia, 1943

C

SCHÜTZENPANZERWAGEN SDKFZ 251/1 AUSF. C

KEY

1. Front armour plate 14.5mm
2. Armoured cover for starter handle
3. Headlights with blackout covers
4. Width indicator bars
5. Pickaxe
6. Armoured radiator cover
7. Motor armour 8mm
8. Motor inspection hatch
8a. Carburettor
9. Air filter
10. Maybach HL 42 TUKRM 4.141 ltr 6 cylinder water-cooled
11. Radio operator's front visor
12. Armoured glass block
13. Radio operator's side visor
14. Front plate 14.5mm
15. Bullet splash guard for MG mount
16. 1.4m rod antenna for Fu.Spr.f radio system
17. 7.92mm MG 34 machine gun with armoured shield
18. Driver's front visor
19. Driver's steering wheel (inverted)
20. Driver's seat
21. Stowage for crew equipment – helmets
22. Stowage for crew equipment – rifles
23. Crew bench seat
24. 7.92mm MG 42 on rear mount
25. Rear door 8mm
26. Fire extinguisher
27. Main fuel tank under floor 160 ltr
28. Spare fuel can
29. Water can
30. Side armour upper 8mm
31. Side armour lower 8mm
32. Notek distance warning light system
33. Stowage bins
34. Starter handle
35. Turn indicator
36. Adjustable idler wheel
37. Road wheel outer and inner pair, 575/50-(505) tyres
38. Road wheel centre pair, 575/48-(505.5) tyres
39. Torsion bars suspension across chassis
40. Lubricated track Typ ZgW or Zpw 5001/280/140
41. 55 links centre guide tooth 280mm wide, 140mm pitch
42. Drive sprocket
43. Rubber track pads
44. Air intake cowl
45. Exhaust manifold
46. Armoured exhaust pipe cover
47. Silencer
48. Mudguard
49. Front wheel
50. Tyres 7.25-20 or 190-18
51. Transverse spring
52. Twin side by side cooling fans
53. Radiator

SPECIFICATIONS

Manufacturer: Adlerwerke, Auto Union, Hanomag, Skoda, MNH, Borgwar
Number built: c. 4,000 in 1941 and 1942
Crew: 2, plus 8 infantry
Combat weight: 9,000kg
Motor: 4.171 ltr Maybach HL 42 TUKRM 6 cylinder
Power output: 100 metric hp at 2,800rpm
Power-to-weight ratio: 14.75 metric hp/tonne
Ground pressure: 0.76kg/cm²
Overall length: 5,800mm
Width: 2,100mm
Height: 1,750mm
Transmission: ZF 6 forward, 1 reverse
Maximum speed (road): 52.5 km/h
Best cruising speed: 38 km/h
Maximum range: 300km at cruising speed
Armament: 2 x 7.92mm MG plus crew weapons
Stowed MG ammunition: 1,425 rounds
Fording depth: 500mm
Trench crossing: 2,000mm

1: SdKfz 251/16 Ausf. C, 1.Panzer-Division, France, summer 1943
2: SdKfz 251/1 Ausf. C, 16.Panzer-Division; Russia, 1943-44

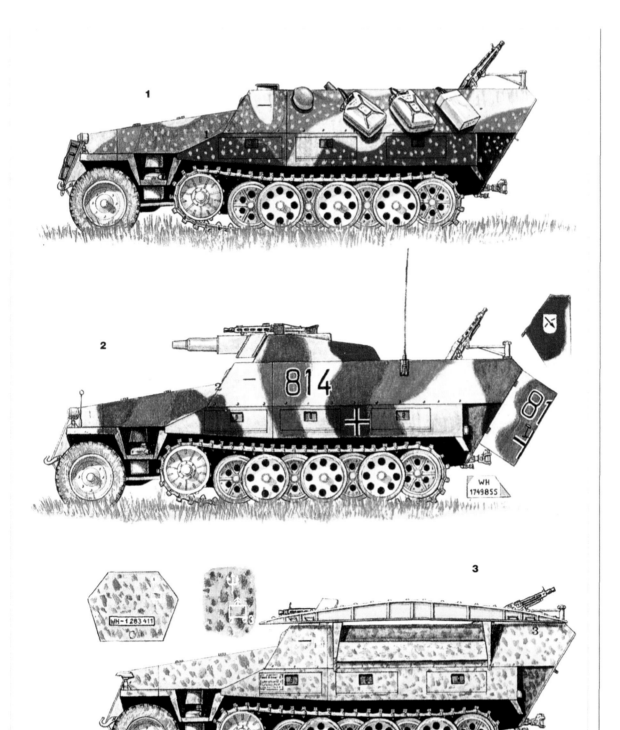

1: SdKfz 251/2 Ausf. D, unidentified unit; Western Europe, autumn 1944
2: SdKfz 251/9 Ausf. D, 20.Panzer-Division; Russia, summer 1944
3: SdKfz 251/7 Ausf. D, Armd.Eng.Bn., 2.Panzer-Division; France, 1944

F

1: SdKfz 251/1 Ausf. D rocket launcher, unidentified unit; Russia, spring 1944
2: SdKfz 251/8 Ausf. D ambulance, Fallschirm-Pz-Div. 'Hermann Goring'; Italy, 1944
3: SdKfz 251/21 Ausf. D captured by US 87th Inf.Div., early 1945

TRAINING AND ORGANISATION

Training during the pre-war and early wartime periods was lavish by most contemporary standards. The progressive leaders of the German Army regarded the Panzer Division as the 'queen of battle', and efforts to improve the tactics and the effectiveness of the armoured formations were given a high priority. Assignment to an armoured infantry regiment was a mark of excellence and, initially at least, these men were carefully chosen from the best troops and recruits.

Initial training was similar to that of the mass of the infantry, and this standard of instruction was very high. The armoured infantry recruits then entered a specialist phase of their training, during which they learned the special tactics involved in a combined assault. Tactics did change considerably during the early war years, because initially there were few armoured carriers available and unarmoured infantry formations were not able to stay as close to the tanks as the armoured groups.

Training covered phases of the assault, advancing with armoured units; reconnaissance, tank-infantry co-operation, and various tactics of securing ground and enemy positions overrun by the tank units. Initial training made use of dummy tanks mounted on light automobiles, but advanced training included operations with light tanks assigned to the training schools. In addition, the Panzer Divisions had training operations for new troops to indoctrinate them as they joined the various line companies.

The 'Schützen' (rifle infantry) regiments were organised on the same lines as the regiments in infantry divisions. Each regiment was composed of two battalions; each battalion had three rifle companies and a heavy support company. A company was composed of three rifle platoons, and these platoons each contained three rifle squads or sections (Gruppen). The SdKfz 251 was designed to carry a ten-man squad or section, and provide a measure of fire support for the section during dismounted engagements.

Each section in an armoured infantry platoon was equipped with two MG34 light machine guns (one with a heavy tripod mount), eight Kar98K service rifles, and two MP38 or MP40 machine pistols for the driver and commander. The heavy MG section had two tripod mounts and a special long-range front mount on the vehicle, but was otherwise similar to the normal infantry section.

There were four SdKfz 251s in a platoon. When it became available, the SdKfz 251/10, armed with the 3.7cm PaK36 anti-tank gun, was issued to the platoon leader for additional heavy fire support. In addition to the normal complement of infantry section vehicles, each platoon had a heavy weapons support section. Additional support units were available for special needs, and during the course of the war a number of different formations were used. It should be remembered that this was the full-strength complement. The shortage of SPWs was such that most Panzer units never managed to carry all their infantry in armoured carriers, only the first battalion of a regiment being designated as armoured. The second (motorised) battalion rode in trucks and was often held in reserve, due to the difficulties of protecting the troops without armoured transport in the forward assault areas.

One administrative problem early in the war was that the Schützen regiments were under the overall command of the Inspector of Infantry, while the tank units were under the Inspector of Armour Troops (Panzertruppe). In July 1942 the Schützen formations were redesignated Panzergrenadiers – largely for morale purposes, as grenadiers had been élite units in the Imperial German Army. However, this redesignation also transferred overall control of the Panzergrenadiers to the Inspector of Armour Troops and thus simplified chains of command. Considering that assault guns were under the Inspector of Artillery, and that most Flak troops were in attached Luftwaffe units, the commanders of the Panzer Divisions were no doubt grateful for the elimination of yet another conflict of authority.

The SdKfz 251/8 was an armoured ambulance, some being purpose-built, and others modified to this layout in the field. This example, in overall grey paint heavily coated with pale dust and mud, served with the Tiger tank battalion sPzAbt. 501 in Tunisia in spring 1943. The two sand-yellow jerrycans on the rear racks bear the white cross marking indicating that they contained water.

As a complement to the full Panzer Divisions, the Germans created a second type of armoured formation, the Panzergrenadier Division. The early Panzergrenadier formations were, in most cases, converted from existing motorised infantry divisions. The Panzergrenadier Division contained two regiments of Panzergrenadier 'armoured' infantry troops, but still with only one battalion in each regiment equipped with SdKfz 251s and the other battalions with trucks. Instead of the full Panzer Regiment of a Panzer Division, there was only one tank battalion, generally equipped with PzKpfw III and IV medium tanks.

Panzergrenadier Divisions allowed additional armoured units to be placed into service without as much pressure on tank production as whole Panzer Divisions would have caused. Later on, this was especially true of Panther production, which had not kept up with the original schedule. The PzKpfw IV was a good support tank and, in its late war configuration, was capable of dealing with most Allied tanks on an equal footing. In 1942 the PzKpfw III with the 5cm L/60 long gun was still a very useful vehicle.

Panzergrenadier Divisions were ideally suited for the armoured assault rôle. Though 'light' in tanks, they possessed enough armour to engage and overwhelm most enemy infantry and isolated armour units.

Column of 251 Ausf. C half-tracks in Russia 1943. The nearest vehicle is a late example of the 251/10 platoon commander's track with 3.7cm anti-tank gun mounted. Most of the shield was removed from later vehicles, leaving only a low strip at the left of the breech to protect the gunner; the commander used a binocular spotting telescope and was not directly exposed to enemy fire.

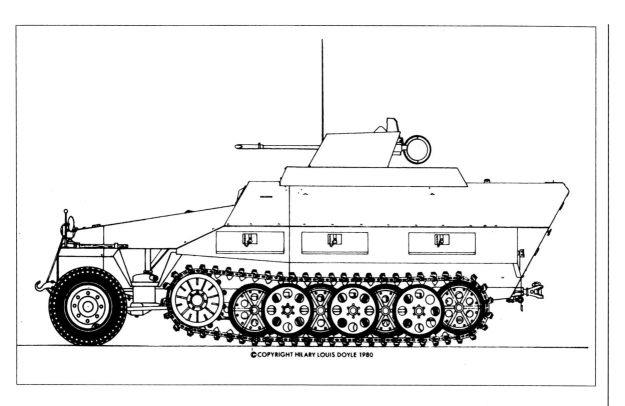

©COPYRIGHT HILARY LOUIS DOYLE 1980

SPW (Drilling MG 151 S) (Gërat 921) SdKfz 251/21.
(© H.L. Doyle)

In the defensive rôle later in the war, they supplemented the firepower of the Panzer Divisions and provided a reserve of strength that was often crucial.

By 1943, under Guderian's aegis, training for Panzergrenadiers had been expanded to include newly developed tactics, and with rather more emphasis on defensive manoeuvres in co-operation with armour. These included support of tank units during counter-attacks, attacking the enemy's exposed flanks, securing important defensive objectives and securing the most advantageous defensive perimeter. This mid-war period marked the zenith in the fortunes of the Panzergrenadiers.

1944 saw the introduction of new weapons and improved versions of existing equipment, such as the Panther Ausf. G and PzKpfw IV Ausf. J. The more ambitious plans to build new SPW designs to replace the SdKfz 250 and 251 were gradually delayed and then abandoned. Thus, the SdKfz 251 Ausf. D, as the final production version, was the vehicle the Panzergrenadiers rode in the retreat across France and to final defeat in 1945. As 1944 passed, increasing shortages and more severe disruption of many daylight activities combined to reduce the effectiveness of the training. In addition, the serious losses of personnel in Russia and, to a lesser extent, France led the Army to reduce the duration and level of training in order to service as many recruits as possible. By 1945 training had become a very rough affair compared to the 1942 period. Many training schools did maintain the highest standards they possibly could; but the shortages of fuel, ammunition, vehicles, and many other critical supplies inevitably lowered the quality of instruction. Fewer older, experienced troops were in the front-line units, so the newly-trained recruits often had to learn the lessons of combat up in the front lines.

Although some Panzer Divisions and Panzergrenadier Divisions did survive into 1945 with fairly good levels of men and equipment, many units suffered from very high levels of attrition, and a number of Panzergrenadier units had to revert to trucks and even tanks for transport. Production of the SdKfz 251, never great enough to meet all the demands, began to fall off in early 1945 as factories in occupied countries and Germany were bombed or captured by Allied forces.

The vehicle establishments of most German formations were decreased in 1944 and 1945, and generally units did not receive even the reduced number of vehicles. It was not uncommon for a dozen or so tanks and perhaps twice that number of SPWs to represent the armoured complement of a Panzer or Panzergrenadier Division in the spring of 1945, and shortages of fuel often did more to restrict the effective use of the armoured units than did their reduced numbers.

Crew of the 251/7 practising a quick start. Heavily modified from the basic Ausf. C to Luftwaffe specifications, in order to mount the 2cm Flak 38 cannon in a widened body with hydraulically-lowering sides for a quick traverse, this version was produced in very small numbers: it is believed that only ten gun-tracks and two command vehicles were completed. A sequence of photos shows them in service with the 2nd Bn. of the Flak-Regiment 'Hermann Göring'.

TACTICS: ASSAULT

The tactics employed by the Panzer Divisions were well thought out, and efficiently executed under the best of circumstances – good preparation, the element of surprise, and sufficient armoured infantry in SPWs to exploit the gains won by the tanks. More importantly, for much of the war these tactics were sufficiently flexible and effective that they usually worked under less-than-ideal conditions, and occasionally succeeded under appalling circumstances. Where they failed the cause was usually massive enemy opposition especially co-ordinated air cover – which caused such heavy attrition in men and material that the Panzer Divisions no longer had sufficient forces to carry out their assigned tasks.

Since the SPWs were to operate as close to the tanks as possible, the basic tactics for the tanks will necessarily be involved in a discussion of the employment of the SdKfz 251. Under the ideal conditions above, the personnel carriers were part of a combined force which in many ways was more than the sum of its parts.

The basic tactical objective of a Panzer or Panzergrenadier Division was to concentrate at a weak point in the enemy's lines a sufficient number of aggressively employed tanks and support troops to break through the enemy front, to spread out to encircle strongpoints and troop concentrations, and to hold open a corridor through which additional armoured and support units could move to expand the breakthrough and repeat the process in the enemy's rear support positions and at other points in the front lines.

The initial operation in an offensive was battlefield reconnaissance. The Panzer Aufklärungs Abteilung (armoured reconnaissance battalion) was responsible for local reconnaissance for a Panzer or Panzergrenadier Division. Using armoured cars, half-tracks, and other vehicles, the reconnaissance detachments probed enemy positions or observed enemy forces. They were also responsible for locating suitable terrain features for the armoured advance, and the placement of artillery and anti-tank guns; and for locating fording areas across streams or suitable positions for building bridges or launching assault boats during an attack.[1]

M. Flammpanzerwagen (SdKfz 251/16). (© H.L. Doyle)

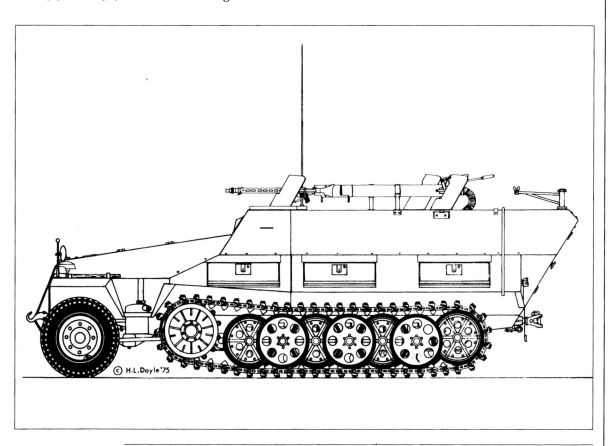

[1]See detailed accounts in the forthcoming title New Vanguard 29, *German Armoured Cars and Reconnaissance Half-Tracks 1939-45.*

The use of combined arms in the assault was critical to German tactics. As early as the Polish campaign, the Germans learned that direct tank assaults against effective anti-tank defences resulted in heavy losses. Later events demonstrated that even large formations of tanks could not achieve a breakthrough when opposed by anti-tank guns unless assisted by Assault Artillery and Panzergrenadiers. Thus, the mobility and armour protection for the Panzergrenadiers was improved as much as possible to allow the infantry to operate up with the armour during an attack.

There were several types of attacks: flank attack, frontal attack, envelopment (combination flank and frontal assaults), wing (against the ends of the enemy's main frontal positions) and encirclement, in which the main attacking force bypasses the enemy positions on a flank, then sweeps around from the rear to manoeuvre the enemy from his prepared positions and disrupt his defences. However, within variables caused by terrain, deployment of the enemy, and resources available for the assault, all these attack plans used very similar tank/infantry tactics. Tanks were intended to break through the front line positions and attack the enemy artillery and command positions. The infantry was to assist the tanks and, in particular, to destroy enemy anti-tank weapons. Enemy tanks were countered by German anti-tank guns, usually self-propelled in the front units of the assault.

An assault was spearheaded by a Panzer regiment (or battalion, in the case of a Panzergrenadier division). Earlier in the war, the standard form of the attack was composed of three waves; though there were variations, the basic tactic was consistent. The first wave was composed of tanks as the forward line of movement. One commonly used formation was the 'blunt wedge'. In this advance, two tank companies of a battalion were lined up abreast; each company was spread to cover about 450 to 500 metres of front line, with about 200 to 300 metres between them. Battalion headquarters was about 500 metres behind the lead tanks, and the third and fourth companies, as reserves, trailed in file (or double file) behind battalion HQ, the rearmost tanks about 900 to 1000 metres behind the HQ troops.

The lead tank companies advanced to the enemy lines and broke through to the artillery and anti-tank defence positions. If resistance developed, the leading companies bypassed it, or the battalion commander could reinforce the tanks with his remaining companies. The tanks advanced in steps, using terrain as cover whenever possible. The rear echelons provided fire support for the advance elements. When the leading tanks had advanced to good firing positions, they laid down fire to support the following vehicles as they advanced to the forward positions. This 'leapfrogging' was the standard tactic for tank advance for most of the war.

The second wave provided fire support for the first wave, and consisted of tank units from the first and/or second tank battalions accompanied by a few companies of Panzergrenadiers in SdKfz 251s. The second wave attacked the remaining anti-tank positions, the heavy infantry support weapons, and enemy machine guns which would slow the following infantry advance.

The third wave, consisting of the remainder of the tanks in the second tank battalion and the rest of the Panzergrenadiers, consolidated the gains won by the first waves, mopped up pockets of resistance bypassed in the assault, and provided a reserve for the lead elements as the assault progressed. Most of the Panzergrenadiers in this third wave were motorised infantry in trucks, as the armoured infantry was used in the first and second waves.

During the actual advance the SPWs of the Panzergrenadier companies stayed from 100 to 150 metres behind the tanks. The SPWs provided fire support directed against enemy forward anti-tank weapons or tank-killer infantry and also advised the armour of additional targets for the tanks' heavier guns. In the flank areas, assault guns or self-propelled anti-tank guns provided support and protection for the tanks. SPWs also accompanied the assault guns when necessary, to provide protection against tank-killer teams or concealed anti-tank weapons.

The actual tactics of the Panzergrenadiers depended on the terrain and objectives. Open terrain was crossed as quickly as possible, using artillery to lay HE shells and/or smoke to provide cover and fire support. When possible, the Panzergrenadiers stayed in the vehicles until they were close enough to the enemy to dismount and attack as infantry. The SPWs provided fire support with the vehicle machine guns. In terrain with more cover, platoons of SPWs would advance in stages from one covered position to another, with the leading and following elements providing fire support for each other. Any natural features such as woods or stream beds were used for cover, and every attempt was made to avoid crossing open terrain under direct fire.

In cases where strong anti-tank defences existed or where there were extensive anti-tank obstacles, the Panzergrenadiers led the assault ahead of the tanks. Although the SdKfz 251 was very vulnerable to anti-tank weapons, in many cases enemy gunners waited as long as possible before firing, since they would thus expose their positions. The tanks remained a few hundred metres behind the SPWs and fired on any enemy positions that were spotted.

In situations where rapid advances could be made with good cover, the Panzergrenadiers could clear enemy anti-tank positions with relatively low losses. Across open terrain the tanks and SPWs were more exposed, and often the tanks had to move closer (100 to 200 metres)

ABOVE **Two Ausf. Ds seen in Budapest in summer 1944. One is a 251/3 finished in a striking, interlocked pattern of green and brown over factory yellow; it has the later 'crow's-foot' radio antenna. The other, a 251/6 fitted with both 'crow's-foot' and frame antennae, is painted in a more faded and random slashing of both colours over yellow; and note Korps command pennant in black, white and red on the mudguard.**

LEFT **Rear view of the Ausf. D; note stowage bins acting as track-guards, and protruding T-shaped door lock handle – the straight Ausf. D doors would not stay closed unless locked. This half-track photographed in Normandy in summer 1944 has the divisional sign obliterated, but is probably from 2.Panzer-Division.**

behind the half-tracks to provide more effective support. Though infantry losses were higher in attacking enemy positions ahead of the tanks, this tactic was essential to allow German armour to manoeuvre freely during the penetration and breakthrough phases of the assault.

After the enemy anti-tank troops had been neutralised, the tanks and Panzergrenadiers advanced together in one assault wave. The infantry rode in the SPWs as far as possible, and dismounted to destroy individual pockets of resistance. The Panzergrenadiers' heavy support weapons – mortars and light artillery pieces – were brought up to fire on any newly discovered enemy anti-tank weapons or artillery. At this point in the assault the primary mission of the Panzergrenadiers was to eliminate enemy positions that had survived the first assault wave, and to protect the rear of the armoured formation.

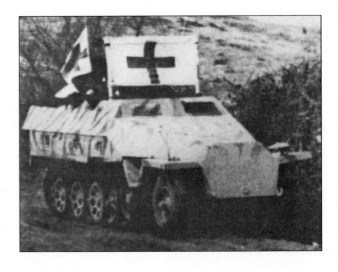

251/8 Ausf. D ambulance of the 'Hermann Göring' Division in Italy 1944 – this is the subject of plate G2.

TACTICS: DEFENCE

German doctrine, like that of the US Army, viewed the objective of a defensive action as a prelude to a counter-attack or to gain time for the marshalling of forces to prepare a new offensive. Thus, the main thrust of German defensive tactics was to halt the enemy's offensive drive, and, if possible, to counter-attack quickly and decisively to break the enemy assault and drive back the assaulting troops. Properly employed under favourable conditions, this tactic could result in a successful new offensive, and even a rout of the enemy forces.

As the war dragged on through 1943-44, however, shortages of men and equipment necessitated revision of the defensive strategy and tactics. More emphasis was placed on fortifications, mine-fields and anti-tank obstacles than previously. The massive counter-attacks by the larger mobile reserves of 1942-43 gave way to smaller local thrusts intended more to keep the enemy off balance than to become a major counter offensive.

The main line of resistance was determined by the local terrain, and was usually developed only after thorough reconnaissance. In 1944, however, the realities of Germany's declining military fortunes resulted in an order that basic work on the defence perimeter had to be started as soon as possible. Reconnaissance thus added detailed information for specific strongpoints or positions, but commanders had to design their defensive lines before all the reconnaissance was completed.

Advanced positions were set 5,000 to 7,000 metres in front of the main line of resistance. Usually, mobile armoured units – reconnaissance detachments, armoured car and half-track platoons, machine guns, and anti-tank guns-were deployed in the advanced positions. They occupied and controlled important terrain features, such as crossroads, bridges, railroads, and high ground. Their primary functions were to report enemy movements and to deceive the enemy as to the location of the

Photographed on display at the Aberdeen Proving Ground, this 251/9 Ausf. D seems to retain the correct markings for a track of an armoured reconnaissance company of 2.Panzer-Division; however, the Aufklärungs-Abteilung normally had only four companies. Of interest is the high, fixed frontal shield behind the 7.5cm L/24 howitzer. The radio, normally in front of the right-hand front seat, was moved to the left rear wall to allow the crew to serve the howitzer, and the antenna mount moved accordingly.

actual main line of resistance. These troops did not hold their positions at all costs, but were to retire to the main positions under cover of German medium artillery.

Because of the flexible nature of German tactics, Panzergrenadiers in SdKfz 251s were sometimes deployed in the advanced positions to reinforce the other detachments. Depending on the terrain and the size of the defending German unit, a platoon or even a company of Panzer-grenadiers might be placed in an advanced position. Their main function was to man the defensive perimeter, sending out patrols and attempting to spot as many enemy positions as possible. They also provided extra firepower during enemy attacks on the advanced positions, and served as the rearguard during withdrawal to the main defensive positions.

Outposts were established about 2,000 to 5,000 metres in front of the main position, and once the advance positions were abandoned, the outposts were the only positions in front of the main line of resistance. In armoured formations outpost positions were manned by Panzergrenadiers, usually from the motorised regiment, supported by reconnaissance detachments and infantry support weapons. By 1944 most reconnaissance units had heavy support companies with SdKfz 251/9 half-tracks carrying 7.5cm L/24 howitzers. These provided fire support for advance and outpost positions. Outpost positions were chosen to provide adequate cover for the deployed units, good fields of fire, and safe routes for withdrawal. Units generally established positions at the edges of woods, in villages and hedgerows, and on hills.

Outpost troops supported small local attacks intended to keep the enemy off balance and to secure information about enemy forces. When the outpost units were withdrawn under pressure of an enemy assault, their old positions were swept by carefully registered artillery, mortar and machine gun fire to prevent them from being taken and occupied by enemy troops.

In the main line of resistance, defensive positions were carefully chosen and interlocked. Platoon strongpoints were incorporated into company strongpoints, and so on up to the largest unit in the line. Most defensive positions were on the reverse slopes of hills or rolling terrain. Forward slope positions were too vulnerable to early detection by directed heavy artillery fire.

Side view of 215/9 Ausf. D – the howitzer is obscured by the background in this blurred photograph. Later production versions sacrificed a low profile for simplicity of construction; the howitzer was mounted higher, on the cab roof, rather than being 'countersunk' into the front plate.

Panzergrenadier units generally camouflaged their vehicles thoroughly in prepared positions. Deployment in heavy woods was not usual when time and materials were in short supply, since occupying woods requires more defensive strength, because of reduced mobility and poor observation. However, use was made of heavy woods when time allowed, since the extensive cover provided the same advantages as reverse slopes in hiding positions from the enemy. Mobile units, however, often used the edges of woods as cover, and SPWs were often placed in heavy brush as an aid to camouflage. This became much more important as the Allies gained air superiority, especially in NW Europe.

In built-up areas – villages, towns and cities – camouflage was equally important. As many vehicles as possible would be hidden in woods, hedgerows, and favourable terrain features, often with heavy netting or foliage, hay, and other materials used as cover. Vehicles hidden in buildings – generally tanks or self-propelled antitank guns – often used parts of the surrounding building as additional camouflage protection.

1944 saw the end of the Luftwaffe's ability to provide effective air cover for German ground units in NW Europe. Most vehicle movement could take place only at night; movement during the day was dangerous and required extraordinary measures. Very heavy foliage camouflage became the accepted practice, and most military routes were lined with hundreds of emergency parking areas, usually under trees or in brush. Some roads even had ready-cut foliage at these emergency pull-ins to cover the tracks and suspensions of parked vehicles.

The experimental Luftwaffe anti-aircraft SdKfz 251, the SdKfz 251/17, and the SdKfz 251/21 were all attempts to provide useful tactical anti-aircraft defences for armoured formations. All failed, for different reasons. The Luftwaffe vehicle was too costly and only trials examples were made. The SdKfz 251/17 suffered from inadequate firepower, and the SdKfz 251/2I – the most effective version – was, like most other German anti-aircraft vehicles, overwhelmed by the hordes of Allied fighter-bombers roaming at will over most of Europe. The US 5in. and British 60lb. air-to-ground rockets proved to be very effective counters to the greater firepower of the 2cm MG151 compared to the .50 Brownings in US fighters.

Even with the loss of effective air cover, German units were capable of presenting effective defences. The Germans applied the same principles

Some blurred but interesting views of formation signs marked on 251s late in the war: here, front and back views of heavily-camouflaged Ausf. Ds of 12.Panzer-Division 'Hitlerjugend' in Normandy. Both have an indistinct camouflage scheme of green and/or brown mottled over yellow and heavy added foliage. The white divisional sign – crossed 'Dietrich' key and Sigrun in shield over oakleaves – appears at front and rear on the right hand side. The front view shows the tactical sign of the armoured radio battalion on the left of the nose; this track has two 'crow's-foot' aerials at the rear hull corners, and an air recognition flag across the engine hood – inappropriate as it seems for Normandy in 1944. The rear view is of a 215/7 – note bridging sections – with the tactical number '440' in black or dark red. It retains an MG34 – most Ausf. Ds had MG42s mounted.

in defence that they did in the assault. The main effort of defence was made opposite the area where the enemy concentrated his attacking forces. In particular, observation posts and reconnaissance units kept enemy forces under observed artillery fire continuously. No matter where an enemy thrust penetrated, artillery fire could follow the advance and try to break the enemy's advancing units.

Panzergrenadiers in SdKfz 251s were normally kept as the reserve for counter-attacks, the forward defensive positions being manned by the motorised Panzergrenadier units. The counter-attack proceeded like a genuine aggressive assault, aimed at stopping the enemy's momentum and turning his lines. Immediate counter-thrusts were directed at enemy penetrations to deny opposing troops the opportunity to hold or consolidate their gains. The SPWs advanced behind or with the tanks, but as the war progressed and shortages became more severe, such counter-attacks were smaller, more localised, and often used assault guns or self-propelled guns. Tanks were in short supply in many units and had to be reserved for major counter-attacks.

For much of the war, German armoured formations had endeavoured to stay out of heavily built-up areas where their tanks and SPWs were vulnerable to attacks by concealed anti-tank guns and infantry. SdKfz 251s were quite vulnerable because of their open tops, but on occasion they were camouflaged in built-up areas and used for fire support or as mobile observation or command posts.

As German units went on to the defensive, however, towns and cities became excellent fortified defensive positions. Tanks and SPWs were considered ineffective as fighting vehicles in a defended town, but they were used as dug-in guns and observation points. Detachments of tanks, assault guns, and SPWs were organised to make surprise counter-attacks against enemy penetrations into the town. Larger, similar mobile reserve battle groups were reserved for bigger counter-attacks. In general, however, most German tanks and SPWs were kept in reserve outside of built-up areas. This reduced their vulnerability to attack and allowed them the freedom of movement so important to the successful employment of armour in the field.

The introduction of the SdKfz 251 Ausf. D, and the expansion of military production under Albert Speer, increased the available numbers of SPWs, and at one time the SdKfz 251 was the most numerous armoured vehicle in the German armed forces. Simultaneously, there were additional attempts to increase the firepower of armoured units, in which the normal establishment of tanks was reduced almost every year.

The SdKfz 251/9, mounting the short 7.5cm L/24 howitzer, was replaced by an improved version which could easily be converted from a standard SPW, though the units produced were manufactured and issued through normal channels. Nonetheless, the greatly reduced work requirement allowed these support vehicles to be produced far more easily and cheaply. Because of a continuing shortage of self-propelled anti-tank guns, the SdKfz 251 was adapted to carry the 7.5cm PaK40, and was assigned to reconnaissance battalions. In the few units which received the /22 model, it supplemented the earlier /9 with the short 7.5cm L/24 howitzer. It was overloaded to some extent, but the SdKfz 251/22 was an effective weapon when used from ambush, especially in the traditional forward defence positions usually manned by reconnaissance units. The /22 had a fairly high silhouette, though it was much lower than many self-propelled PaK40 mounts. However, it was vastly more effective than the SdKfz 251/9 with the short howitzer. Firing at enemy armour was often delayed until the tanks were only 300 metres away, to ensure quick destruction of the targets. The PaK40 could, if necessary, engage armour at ranges of 1,500 metres or more. This greater range capability allowed more flexibility in positioning these anti-tank vehicles.

SERVICEABILITY

The relatively complex design of the main suspension led to increased maintenance requirements. The track links were connected with steel pins riding in needle bearings, and each shoe had an oil reservoir for the bearings. Periodically, the level of lubricant had to be checked for every link. In addition, leaks had to be repaired promptly if possible. Sand or dirt mixed with leaking oil or grease could form an abrasive compound which could quickly damage the seals and track pins. The front axle beam and wheels were not as robust as the driven front axle on US half-tracks and the lack of a powered axle reduced the cross-country performance somewhat. Some drivers found the angled steering wheel awkward, and vision – as in most armoured vehicles – left much to be desired, even when 'opened up'.

The Maybach HL 42 engine was somewhat underpowered for the SdKfz 251, though tests with a US M3 half-track showed that this lack of

SdKfz 251/4 Ausf. D of 5.SS-Panzer-Division 'Wiking' towing a 7.5cm PaK40 anti-tank gun on the Eastern Front, 1944-45. The shortage of SP weapons in many units forced the retention of towed guns until the end of the war. The tactical sign on the right rear hull seems to indicate the motorised, rather than the armoured, battalion of this Panzergrenadier regiment, which must have been either 'Germania' or 'Westland' at this date. The divisional sign of a white 'mobile' swastika in circular form appears within a shield to the left of the white-trimmed black vehicle number '2533'.

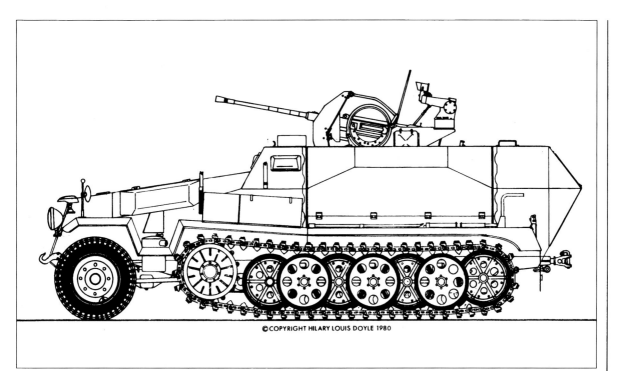

©COPYRIGHT HILARY LOUIS DOYLE 1980

M SPW (2 Flak)
Luftwaffenausfuhrung.
(© H.L. Doyle)

power was not critical in most circumstances. The M3 half-track was generally superior on roads and in flat or rolling country. In rougher going, the SdKfz 251's more sophisticated suspension proved better, being especially superior in crossing ditches or rough stream banks. The rollers fitted to many Allied M2/M3 half-tracks did give an advantage in climbing a vertical obstacle, but the SdKfz 251 was much less likely to get stuck at the crest, since the 3/4 length track run could support the weight of the whole vehicle. Later in the war some SdKfz 251s were fitted with all-metal tracks without the rubber pads. While effective in cross-country use, they caused too much vibration for use on paved roads and were replaced with the original tracks.

The war in Russia brought new problems. All German vehicles suffered from the effects of cold. Engine oil congealed, then froze; gearboxes stuck solid, and wheel bearings froze. A great deal of effort had to be devoted to working out solutions to these – and other – problems. The use of heaters and even small fires to heat engine crank-cases was widespread, and most vehicles were supplied with heating torches to deal with frozen or jammed components. Engine wear was greatly increased because the thicker oil did not lubricate well until the engine had warmed up. Cold metal parts failed more easily, and were under greater strain because of stiff lubricants. Many units using the standard half-tracks with interleaved road-wheels learned that snow and ice left in the suspensions overnight could freeze solid, resulting in stranded vehicles or broken tracks when the crews attempted to move out in the morning. The interleaved wheel design also resulted in side loads on the bearings during turns and in traversing rough ground, and maintenance had to be done on a fairly regular basis to ensure reliable performance. The transmission and final drive unit were very similar to simpler tank powertrains, and the clutch and brake steering components required adjustment and maintenance more often than the simpler truck differential on the M2/M3 half-tracks.

Operations in the desert of North Africa and the hot dusty plains of southern Russia required additional maintenance procedures. The primary problem was lack of proper cooling, but the SdKfz 251 had a good cooling system layout and overheating was not generally a serious problem. Dust infiltration was an equally serious problem, and months of development and improvements to oil filters were needed to increase serviceability. Even with improved filters, frequent oil changes were required, and engines and transmissions wore out faster than the norm in northern Europe.

The desert climate and terrain were extremely harsh on wheels, tyres and suspensions. The Germans often covered the tyres on vehicles when stopped, since excessive heat could devulcanise the rubber. Tyre pressures were checked often because of heat build-up during marches. The limestone outcroppings in much of the African desert ruined the rubber roadwheel tyres and rubber track pads. The dust and sand necessitated frequent cleaning of air filters and all moving parts.

In spite of its more complex components, the SdKfz 251 proved a most useful vehicle. The basic vehicle was adaptable to a variety of rôles, and performed most of these functions satisfactorily. Allied experience with captured SdKfz 251s appears to have been mixed. Many units, like the US 3rd Army, evaluated the SPW and found it deficient in a number of areas, especially in durability. The massive M2/M3 half-tracks were better suited to the aggressive driving style of the Americans. On the other hand, a number of US and British units captured numbers of SdKfz 251s and cheerfully used them until they broke down, at which point the disabled vehicles were usually pushed off the road and left to the depredations of souvenir hunters and scavengers. Because of their distinctive shape, captured German SPWs were usually marked with prominent white stars.

Post-war use of the SdKfz 251 was generally limited to areas liberated from German occupation near the end of the war. During the early post-war years, surplus Allied military vehicles began replacing those German vehicles retained for transportation and other uses. The surviving SPWs were usually broken up as scrap, the fate for most German tactical vehicles.

Czechoslovakia was producing the SdKfz 251 Ausf. D and, after the end of the war, production continued for the Czech Army. Various changes were made and the final version, the OT-810, had a redesigned body, a diesel engine and a modified suspension with cast steel single pin tracks without the distinctive rubber pads. Versions of the OT-810 have served since its introduction in the early 1960s.

The SdKfz 251 proved the concept of a competent cross-country tactical vehicle for armoured infantry units. The successes of the Panzer Divisions led to adaptations and outright copying of the German tactics by the Allied powers. These revitalised forces drove the German troops into their homeland, using tactics very similar to those of the Panzer and Panzergrenadier divisions. Most modern armies owe their basic tactics of armour infantry co-operation to the early German successes, and the SdKfz 251 deserves a place in history as an integral part of those

successful actions.

THE PLATES

A1: SDKFZ 251/1 AUSF. A, 10TH COMPANY, SCHÜTZEN REGIMENT 1, 1.PANZER-DIVISION; FRANCE, 1940

The typical appearance of the early SPW, finished in overall 'Panzer grey'. Note the upper half of the rear hull doors painted white as an air identification measure; and the tactical markings of 10th Company, together with the oakleaf divisional emblem. The use of sandbags to protect the front gunner was common before the introduction of the armour shield.

A2: SDKFZ 251/6 AUSF. C., HQ 9.PANZER-DIVISION; RUSSIA, 1941

The conspicuous frame antenna was later replaced by the 'crow's-foot' rod antenna. Note command marking and divisional sign on front plate.

A3: SDKFZ 251/3 AUSF. B., LUFTWAFFE 'FLIVO' DEUTSCHES AFRIKAKORPS; LIBYA, 1942

Distinguished by its tall telescopic rod antenna, this vehicle was used by Luftwaffe ground control officers providing the communications link between DAK units and the air force units supporting them. Painted in all-over 1941-42 yellow-brown, the half-track appears to bear a small insignia of a red map of Africa on a white panel on the rear quarter.

B1: SDKFZ 251/3 AUSF. B, 3.PANZER DIVISION, RUSSIA, 1942

Though lacking distinctive markings, this vehicle is interesting in having the 2.8cm tapered-bore Panzerbuchse anti-tank gun mounted in place of the forward MG34. Note the appliqué armour plates on the driver's front plate; and the side hull racks for spare track links.

B2: SDKFZ 251/1 AUSF. C, 24.PANZER-DIVISION; RUSSIA, 1942

The forward MG34 appears to be fitted on the heavy mount. This vehicle is almost completely covered in a coating of mud, and a streaked effect is visible on the side bins.

C1: SDKFZ 251/3 AUSF. B, 21.PANZER-DIVISION, DEUTSCHES AFRIKAKORPS; LIBYA, 1941

There was a shortage of sand-colour paint in the spring and early summer of 1941, and 'expedient' colour schemes were observed, with partial application of paint, or even of water-and-sand mud over the factory grey finish. This vehicle is unusual in carrying the top section of the collapsible gun mast as a radio antenna. Note small white DAK emblem on side of engine housing.

C2: SDKFZ 251/6 AUSF. C, HQ PANZER-GRENADIER-REGT. 'GROSSDEUTSCHLAND'; RUSSIA, 1943

Finished in the overall dark yellow factory paint scheme of German armoured vehicles from early 1943 onwards, this SPW bears the white helmet sign of the Panzer-Division 'GD'; and the white '01' which identified the command vehicle of Oberst Lorenz, the regimental commander, together with command pennant flown from the mudguard.

C3: SDKFZ 251/10 AUSF.C, UNIDENTIFIED UNIT; NORTH RUSSIA, 1943

The supply of white camouflage paint was more reliable from winter 1942-43 onwards than it had been in the first winter of the campaign. Many vehicles were completely overpainted, with no attempt made to retain national or tactical markings which might give enemy weapons crews an aiming point. On this SPW only the individual vehicle name 'Baden' has been preserved.

D: SDKFZ 251/1 AUSF. C, 'GROSSDEUTSCHLAND' DIVISION

The vehicle illustrated is a Mittlerer Schützenpanzerwagen (SdKfz 251/1) Ausf. C; it is the definitive model of the type – the standard German armoured troop carrier. The 'C' was the most common production model from 1941-43. This one is armed with an MG34 machine gun in front and an MG42 machine gun in the rear. The markings of the vehicle indicate a 251/1 Ausf. C of the 'Grossdeutschland' Division, c. 1942-43. The white 'Stahlhelm' (steel helmet) is the tactical emblem for this Panzergrenadier-Division which was one of the best formations of the Wehrmacht and fought almost entirely on the Eastern Front.

E1: SDKFZ 251/16 AUSF. C, 1.PANZER-DIVISION; FRANCE, SUMMER 1943

Between January and June 1943 this division was refitting in France, and received many replacement vehicles, including this factory-fresh flamethrower Ausf. C in unblemished condition and overall dark yellow paintwork. Note divisional oakleaf sign on front – and, presumably, rear – quarter.

E2: SDKFZ 251/1 AUSF. C, PANZERGRENADIER-REGT. 64, 16. PANZER-DIVISION; RUSSIA, 1943–44

Tactical markings were often painted directly on to the front plate, instead of on a separate plate. This vehicle, in an overall covering of whitewash, bears in red the divisional insignia above the tactical marking of the 6th Company of the division's Panzergrenadier-Regiment 64.

F1: SDKFZ 251/2 AUSF. D, UNIDENTIFIED UNIT; WESTERN FRONT, AUTUMN 1944

The 'ambush' colour scheme of three shades in a pattern intended to simulate sunlight dappled through trees was fairly unusual for a half-track. Note, however, that this is a mortar-carrier vehicle, which would logically operate in semi-static concealed positions and thus required a more careful camouflage scheme than the usual run of troop carriers.

F2: SDKFZ 251/9 AUSF. D, 20.PANZER-DIVISION; RUSSIA, SUMMER 1944

This late-production vehicle, with the 7.5cm howitzer mounted, bears a tactical number indicating 4th vehicle, 1st Platoon, 8th Company in the manner of tank tactical numbers. Note the divisional sign on the rear hull quarter, perhaps repeated on the front plate. The three standard issue paint colours are used here in a 'cloud' pattern.

F3: SDKFZ 251/7 AUSF. D, ARMOURED ENGINEER BATTALION, 2. PANZER-DIVISION; FRANCE, 1944

In contrast, the rather less effective mottled pattern of the same three colours is used here. The division's trident emblem, and the tactical marking of the battalion's 3rd Company, are marked on front, rear, and side surfaces, the latter just visible beside the driver's side vision slot. The lack of the national cross is notable.

G1: SDKFZ 251/1 AUSF. D, MIT WUFRAHMEN, UNIDENTIFIED UNIT; RUSSIA, SPRING 1944

Unidentified except by the individual vehicle name 'Gerti', this 251/1 Ausf. D has the six 28cm rocket launchers mounted along the hull sides. The rocket crates, being expendable, appeared in a number of colours. The 'cloud' pattern is again evident; dark green and brown pastes were issued, and diluted and applied at unit level over the factory finish of dark yellow.

G2: SDKFZ 251/8 AUSF. D AMBULANCE, FALLSCHIRMPANZER-DIVISION 'HERMANN GÖRING'; ITALY, 1944

Colour scheme displayed by a purpose-built ambulance vehicle of the Luftwaffe's premier armoured formation, photographed near Monte Cassino early in 1944. Other vehicles were converted to this role in the field. The large Red Cross flags were common; painted markings were often obscured by mud or dust, and were hard to distinguish at a distance.

G3: SDKFZ 251/21 AUSF. D, UNIDENTIFIED UNIT; EUROPE, 1945

Typical of the very plain finish of many late-war vehicles, this SPW captured intact in 'march order' by the US 87th Infantry Division bears only a black railway loading label on the forward stowage bin door.

INDEX